O Lord, you have always been our home.
Before you created the hills or brought
the world into being, you were eternally God,
and will be God forever.

Psalms 90:1-2

The Gift of an

All Catholic Christmas

The story of the First Christmas taken from the Holy Bible.
Featuring your favorite Holy Christmas Songs.

ANGELA TRUNKETT & LAURA BETHEL

*She will have a son,
and you will name him Jesus -
because he will save his
people from their sins."*

Matthew 1:21

The Gift of an
All Catholic Christmas

This very day in David's town your Savior was born — Christ the Lord!

Luke 2:11

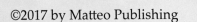

Give thanks to the Lord,
proclaim his greatness;
tell the nations what he has done.

Psalms 105:1

The Gift of an
All Catholic Christmas

Dedication

This book is dedicated to the lost, the fallen away, the worldly and to those
who are caught up in the busy affairs of life. This book is also dedicated
to practicing Catholics who pray and attend mass on Sundays. It is a refresher
and reminder for people who used to be Catholic and those who haven't
been taught their faith or for whatever reason no longer believe.

A child is born to us!
A son is given to us!
And he will be our ruler.
He will be called, "Wonderful Counselor,"
"Mighty God," "Eternal Father,"
"Prince of Peace"

Isaiah 9:6

The Gift of an All-Catholic Christmas

Table of Contents

But the angel said to them,
"Don't be afraid! I am here with good news for you,
which will bring great joy to all the people. This very day in David's town
your Savior was born-Christ the Lord!
And this is what will prove it to you: you will find a baby
wrapped in cloths and lying in a manger." Suddenly a great army
of heaven's angels appeared with the angel, singing praises to God:
"Glory to God in the highest heaven, and peace on
earth to those with whom he is pleased!"

Luke 2: 10-14

The Gift of an All Catholic Christmas

Introduction

As it is written in the book of the prophet Isaiah:

"Someone is shouting in the desert:
'Get the road ready for the Lord;
make a straight path for him to travel!
Every valley must be filled up,
every hill and mountain leveled off.
The winding roads must be made straight,
and the rough paths made smooth.
All mankind will see God's salvation!'"

Luke 3: 4-6

Christmas is more than a day it is a season. It begins with Advent which starts four Sundays before Christmas day. The season ends with the Epiphany, the Feast of the Magi on the Sunday between the second and eighth of January. Advent is a time of preparation and repentance.

As John the Baptist calls us to repent. Matthew 3:2 *"Turn away from your sins,"* he said, *"because the Kingdom of heaven is near!"*

Advent Prayer

Father, in the wilderness of the Jordan You sent a messenger to prepare people's hearts for the coming of Your Son. Help me to hear His words and repent of my sins, so that I may clearly see the way to walk, the truth to speak, and the life to live for Him, our Lord Jesus Christ. Amen.

Christmas is the time that God gives us to be quiet and reflect, to forgive and ask for forgiveness. A special time for letting go of past hurts and injustices. This is an opportunity for welcoming and opening our homes and our hearts. It is a reason to let in the light that casts out the darkness. It is only God that gives us the gift of truth and the promise of peace. This is the season of coming home and coming back.

There is nothing new in this book; the words are ancient, handed down from the beginning of time. They are God's Words, straight from the Bible. God's Words, like God Himself, are the same yesterday, today, and tomorrow. The Word of God is not new, yet it is always alive and vibrant with newness.

God's Word speaks to the inner most cells of our hearts. It penetrates our being; it heals and comforts. It makes us feel again. The word of God brings us home to truth and love.

God made the universe and each one of us. He wanted us to live in perfect happiness with Him. He gave us free will because He did not want us to be slaves. When Adam and Eve first sinned, the forces of evil were unleashed upon humanity. Due to our weak nature, sin seems attractive in that it falsely promises freedom, power, wealth and immortality.

Once caught in its snarls what one finds is: slavery to sin, oppression, cruelty, immorality, paganism, worship of idols, sexual perversity, addictions, bondage, sickness, expendability of human life, endless wars, constant turmoil and death. This was how the world was at the time Jesus was born.

God knew our helplessness. Temptation seemed to be too much for our wounded humanness. God saw this and still loved us. His mercy and compassion are endless. Although all humanity would suffer from the evil in the world, God in His Goodness, gave us hope.

God never meant for us to suffer or to die. Adam and Eve lived in a garden of paradise surrounded with beauty and peace. Ever since "The Fall", which was the disobedience of man that caused human beings to have a fallen nature, all people are born with original sin on their souls. Through the Sacrament of Baptism alone we are washed clean of the original sin on our souls.

God loved us so much that He made another way for us to live.

"I will make you and the woman hate each other; her offspring and yours will always be enemies. Her offspring will crush your head, and you will bite their heel."

Genesis 3:15

God is talking to the devil. "The woman" is The Blessed Virgin Mary whose offspring is Jesus, the Son of God who crushes the head of the devil, so the devil has no more power over humanity.

God, in His Divine Providence chose Saint Joseph, who was the descendant of David, to be the spouse of the Blessed Virgin Mary. He was obedient and in all humility said, 'yes', without questioning. Next to our Blessed Mother, he was the greatest of saints. His 'yes' changed the world. He was head of the Holy Family - their protector and provider. Saint Joseph was the foster father of Jesus. He was also Jesus's teacher and he taught by example.

God, in His Divine Providence, chose Mary, above all women to be the Mother of God. Our Blessed Mother Mary is the Immaculate Conception. She alone, out of all humanity was conceived without original sin.

The Blessed Virgin Mary in all humility was obedient to God. She had free will as we all do and without understanding she freely said yes to God. Her 'yes' changed the world.

Our Christian lineage and history are found through Mary. By her fidelity and obedience, God used her to bring salvation to mankind through the incarnation of Christ, the Son of God. The Blessed Virgin Mary is greater than all the saints. She is the Mother of God.

God used Angels as messengers.

God used His Angel Gabriel to announce the news to Zechariah of Elizabeth's miraculous pregnancy in her old age. God sent the Angel Gabriel to the Virgin Mary to announce that God has greatly blessed her and she will become pregnant and give birth to a son and she will name him Jesus.

Mary and Joseph were promised in marriage to each other. They did not have relations so Joseph did not know what to think of Mary's pregnancy. In his heart he knew she was good and pure. Then an Angel of The Lord appeared in a dream to Joseph informing him of God's plan and directing him to marry her. After Jesus was born an Angel of the Lord instructed Joseph to escape to Egypt because King Herod wanted to kill the Holy Child. After King Herod's death an Angel of The Lord appeared again in a dream to Joseph and instructed him to return home to the land of Israel.

Then, there were a multitude of angels that appeared to the shepherds in the fields to announce the birth of Christ the King.

God promised He would send His only Son, who would come into the world as a baby. He would be true God and true Man. From the beginning God chose Mary to be the Mother of God and Joseph to be His foster father. It would be a virgin birth; he would be conceived by the Holy Spirit, born of the Virgin Mary, and become man. This Christmas mystery is stated in "The Apostle's Creed", which is the essence of Catholicism.

Apostle's Creed

*I believe in God, the Father almighty, creator of heaven and
earth. I believe in Jesus Christ, his only Son, our Lord.
He was conceived by the power of the Holy Spirit and born of
the Virgin Mary. He suffered under Pontius Pilate, was
crucified, died, and was buried. He descended into hell.
On the third day He rose again. He ascended into heaven
and is seated at the right hand of the Father. He will come
again to judge the living and the dead.*

*I believe in the Holy Spirit, the Holy Catholic Church,
the communion of saints, the forgiveness of sins,
the resurrection of the body, and the life everlasting.
Amen.*

$\mathcal{G}$od promised that He would send His people a Savior, the Son of God. From the beginning of time God spoke through His prophets of the coming of Christ and what signs to look for. Generation after generation believed these words. They waited and longed for the day when the Savior would come and they would have peace. When the Savior, who was Jesus Christ did come, He spoke these very words:

"Peace is what I leave with you; It is my own peace
that I give you. I do not give it as the world does.
Do not be worried and upset; do not be afraid."

John 14:27

The world is not what it promises. True peace, joy and acceptance come only through Jesus Christ who humbled himself and entered the world as a defenseless little baby so that we might accept Him in our hearts.

The scripture was fulfilled, for not only the people of Israel, but for all mankind. Jesus Christ is the Savior of the world and if people let Jesus into their hearts, He will set them free. He will give them peace; He will fill their days with love and joy beyond understanding.

Finally, after centuries of waiting, the Lord, Jesus Christ came into the world. He was born in the quiet of a very cold night in the little town of Bethlehem called the City of David. He was born in the humbleness of a stable and in the company of animals. His mother was the Blessed Virgin Mary and His father was Saint Joseph. To the world they appeared to be just an ordinary couple named Mary and Joseph, two young humble people who loved God and were open to His Will. They were chosen to be the parents of our Lord and Savior - Jesus Christ. The Son of God became human like us and nothing would ever be the same again.

*"A virgin will become pregnant and have a son,
and he will be called Immanuel" (which means, "God is with us").*

Matthew 1:23

The following pages have passages taken from the Old Testament and the New Testament of the Holy Bible. The Holy Bible is the inspired Word of God from the beginning of time. It is also a historic account of all creation and mankind. In the Old Testament the prophecies of the coming of Jesus are written. The birth of Jesus is found in the New Testament along with His miracles and teachings.

The story of the first Christmas is taken from the Holy Bible and therefore written in God's words. It is a true story of heroic self-sacrifice, great humility and the obedience to God's call. The Christmas Story is taken from the Gospels of Matthew, Luke and John.

This is the word of the Lord

Before the world was created,
the Word already existed;
he was with God, and he was the same as God.
From the very beginning
the Word was with God.
Through him God made all things;
not one thing in all creation
was made without him.
The Word was the source of life,
and this life brought light to mankind.
The light shines in the darkness, and the darkness
has never put it out.

John 1:1-5

The Holy Bible

The Angel of

Our Lord

Elizabeth

Zechariah

The Child

The Blessed

Virgin Mary

Jesus

Saint Joseph

Simeon

The Three Kings

from the East

King Herod

The Holy Bible

ISAIAH 9: 1-6 THE FUTURE KING

The land of the tribes of Zebulun and Naphtali was once disgraced, but the future will bring honor to this region, from the Mediterranean eastward to the land on the other side of the Jordan, and even to Galilee itself, where the foreigners live. The people who walked in darkness have seen a great light. They lived in a land of shadows, but now light is shining on them. You have given them great joy, Lord; You have made them happy. They rejoice in what you have done, as people rejoice when they harvest grain or when they divide captured wealth. For you have broken the yoke that burdened them and the rod that beat their shoulders. You have defeated the nation that oppressed and exploited your people, just as you defeated the army of Midian long ago. The boots of the invading army and all their bloodstained clothing will be destroyed by fire.

A child is born to us!
A son is given to us!
And he will be our ruler.
He will be called, "Wonderful Counselor,"
"Mighty God," "Eternal Father,"
"Prince of Peace."

LUKE 1: 5-17
THE BIRTH OF JOHN THE BAPTIST IS ANNOUNCED

During the time when Herod was king of Judea, there was a priest named Zechariah, who belonged to the priestly order of Abijah. His wife's name was Elizabeth; she also belonged to a priestly family. They both lived good lives in God's sight and obeyed fully all the Lord's laws and commands. They had no children because Elizabeth could not have any, and she and Zechariah were both very old.

One day Zechariah was doing his work as a priest in the Temple, taking his turn in the daily service. According to the custom followed by the priests, he was chosen by lot to burn incense on the altar. So he went into the Temple of the Lord, while the crowd of people outside prayed during the hour when the incense was burned. An angel of the Lord appeared to him, standing at the right side of the altar where the incense was burned. When Zechariah saw him he was alarmed and felt afraid.

But the angel said to him,

"Don't be afraid, Zechariah! God has heard your prayer, and your wife Elizabeth will bear you a son. You are to name him John. How glad and happy you will be, and how happy many others will be when he is born! He will be a great man in the Lord's sight. He must not drink any wine or strong drink. From his very birth he will be filled with The Holy Spirit, and he will bring back many of the people of Israel to the Lord their God. He will go ahead of the Lord, strong and mighty like the prophet Elijah. He will bring fathers and children together again; he will turn disobedient people back to the way of thinking of the righteous; he will get the Lord's people ready for him."

The Holy Bible

LUKE 1: 18-27
THE BIRTH OF JOHN THE BAPTIST IS ANNOUNCED

Zechariah said to the angel,
"How shall I know if this is so?
I am an old man, and my wife is old also."

"I am Gabriel," the angel answered. "I stand in the presence of God, who sent me to speak to you and tell you this good news. But you have not believed my message, which will come true at the right time. Because you have not believed, you will be unable to speak; you will remain silent until the day my promise to you comes true."

In the meantime the people were waiting for Zechariah and wondering why he was spending such a long time in the Temple. When he came out, he could not speak to them, and so they knew that he had seen a vision in the Temple. Unable to say a word, he made signs to them with his hands. When his period of service in the Temple was over, Zechariah went back home.

Some time later his wife Elizabeth became pregnant and did not leave the house for five months.
"Now at last the Lord has helped me,"
she said. "He has taken away my public disgrace!"

THE BIRTH OF JESUS IS ANNOUNCED

In the sixth month of Elizabeth's pregnancy God sent the angel Gabriel to a town in Galilee named Nazareth. He had a message for a girl promised in marriage to a man named Joseph, who was a descendant of King David. The girl's name was Mary.

The Holy Bible

LUKE 1: 28-38
THE BIRTH OF JESIS IS ANNOUNCED

The angel came to her and said,

"Peace be with you! The Lord is with you and has greatly blessed you!"

Mary was deeply troubled by the angel's message, and she wondered what his words meant. The angel said to her,

"Don't be afraid, Mary; God has been gracious to you. You will become pregnant and give birth to a son, and you will name him Jesus. He will be great and will be called the Son of the Most High God. The Lord God will make him a king, as his ancestor David was, and he will be the king of the descendants of Jacob forever; his kingdom will never end!"

Mary said to the angel,

"I am a virgin. How, then, can this be?"

The angel answered, "The Holy Spirit will come on you, and God's power will rest upon you. For this reason the holy child will be called the Son of God. Remember your relative Elizabeth. It is said that she cannot have children, but she herself is now six months pregnant, even though she is very old. For there is nothing that God cannot do."

"I am the Lord's servant," said Mary;
"may it happen to me as you have said."

And the angel left her.

The Holy Bible

LUKE 1: 39-45
MARY VISITS ELIZABETH

Soon afterward Mary got ready and hurried off to a town in the hill country of Judea. She went into Zechariah's house and greeted Elizabeth. When Elizabeth heard Mary's greeting, the baby moved within her. Elizabeth was filled with the Holy Spirit and said in a loud voice,

"You are the most blessed of all women, and blessed is the child you will bear! Why should this great thing happen to me, that my Lord's mother comes to visit me? For as soon as I heard your greeting, the baby within me jumped with gladness. How happy you are to believe that the Lord's message to you will come true!"

LUKE 1: 46-56
MARY'S SONG OF PRAISE

Mary said, "My heart praises the Lord; my soul is glad because of God my Savior, for he has remembered me, his lowly servant! From now on all people will call me happy, because of the great things the Mighty God has done for me. His name is holy; from one generation to another he shows mercy to those who honor him. He has stretched out his mighty arm and scattered the proud with all their plans. He has brought down mighty kings from their thrones, and lifted up the lowly. He has filled the hungry with good things, and sent the rich away with empty hands. He has kept the promise he made to our ancestors, and has come to the help of his servant Israel.
He has remembered to show mercy to Abraham and to all his descendants forever!"

Mary stayed about three months with Elizabeth and then went back home.

The Holy Bible

LUKE 1: 57-66
THE BIRTH OF JOHN THE BAPTIST

The time came for Elizabeth to have her baby, and she gave birth to a son. Her neighbors and relatives heard how wonderfully good the Lord had been to her, and they all rejoiced with her. When the baby was a week old, they came to circumcise him, and they were going to name him Zechariah, after his father.

But his mother said,

"No! His name is to be John."

They said to her, **"But you don't have any relative with that name!"** Then they made signs to his father, asking him what name he would like the boy to have.

Zechariah asked for a writing pad and wrote, **"His name is John."** How surprised they all were! At that moment Zechariah was able to speak again, and he started praising God. The neighbors were all filled with fear, and the news about these things spread through all the hill country of Judea. Everyone who heard of it thought about it and asked, **"What is this child going to be?"** For it was plain that the Lord's power was upon him.

LUKE 1: 67-80

ZECHARIAH'S PROPHECY

John's father Zechariah was filled with the Holy Spirit, and he spoke God's message:

"Let us praise the Lord, the God of Israel!" He has come to the help of his people and has set them free. He has provided for us a mighty Savior, a descendant of his servant David. He promised through his holy prophets long ago that he would save us from our enemies, from the power of all those who hate us.

He said he would show mercy to our ancestors and remember his sacred covenant. With a solemn oath to our ancestor Abraham he promised to rescue us from our enemies and allow us to serve him without fear, so that we might be holy and righteous before him all the days of our life.

"You, my child, will be called a prophet of the Most High God. You will go ahead of the Lord to prepare his road for him, to tell his people that they will be saved by having their sins forgiven. Our God is merciful and tender. He will cause the bright dawn of salvation to rise on us and to shine from heaven on all those who live in the dark shadow of death, to guide our steps into the path of peace."

The child grew and developed in body and spirit. He lived in the desert until the day when he appeared publicly to the people of Israel.

The Holy Bible

MATTHEW 1: 18-25
THE BIRTH OF JESUS CHRIST

This was how the birth of Jesus Christ took place. His mother Mary was engaged to Joseph, but before they were married, she found out that she was going to have a baby by the Holy Spirit. Joseph was a man who always did what was right, but he did not want to disgrace Mary publicly; so he made plans to break the engagement privately. While he was thinking about this, an angel of the Lord appeared to him in a dream and said,

"Joseph, descendant of David, do not be afraid to take Mary to be your wife. For it is by the Holy Spirit that she has conceived. She will have a son, and you will name him Jesus-because he will save his people from their sins."

Now all this happened in order to make come true what the Lord had said through the prophet, **"A virgin will become pregnant and have a son, and he will be called Immanuel"** (which means, **"God is with us"**). So when Joseph woke up, he married Mary, as the angel of the Lord had told him to. But he had no sexual relations with her before she gave birth to her son. And Joseph named him Jesus.

LUKE 2: 1-7
THE BIRTH OF JESUS

At that time Emperor Augustus ordered a census to be taken throughout the Roman Empire. When this first census took place, Quirinius was the governor of Syria. Everyone, then, went to register himself, each to his own hometown. Joseph went from the town of Nazareth in Galilee to the town of Bethlehem in Judea, the birthplace of King David. Joseph went there because he was a descendant of David. He went to register with Mary, who was promised in marriage to him. She was pregnant, and while they were in Bethlehem, the time came for her to have her baby. She gave birth to her first son, wrapped him in cloths and laid him in a manger-there was no room for them to stay in the inn.

LUKE 2: 8-20
THE SHEPHERDS AND THE ANGELS

There were some shepherds in that part of the country who were spending the night in the fields, taking care of their flocks. An angel of the Lord appeared to them, and the glory of the Lord shone over them. They were terribly afraid, but the angel said to them,

"Don't be afraid! I am here with good news for you, which will bring great joy to all the people. This very day in David's town your Savior was born-Christ the Lord! And this is what will prove it to you: you will find a baby wrapped in cloths and lying in a manger." Suddenly a great army of heaven's angels appeared with the angel, singing praises to God:

**"Glory to God in the highest heaven, and peace
on earth to those with whom he is pleased!"**

When the angels went away from them back into heaven, the shepherds said to one another,**"Let's go to Bethlehem and see this thing that has happened, which the Lord has told us."** So they hurried off and found Mary and Joseph and saw the baby lying in the manger. When the shepherds saw him, they told them what the angel had said about the child. All who heard it were amazed at what the shepherds said. Mary remembered all these things and thought deeply about them. The shepherds went back, singing praises to God for all they had heard and seen; it had been just as the angel had told them.

LUKE 2: 21
JESUS IS NAMED

A week later, when the time came for the baby to be circumcised, he was named Jesus, the name which the angel had given him before he had been conceived.

The Holy Bible

LUKE 2: 22-38
JESUS IS PRESENTED IN THE TEMPLE

The time came for Joseph and Mary to perform the ceremony of purification, as the Law of Moses commanded. So they took the child to Jerusalem to present him to the Lord, as it is written in the law of the Lord:

"Every first-born male is to be dedicated to the Lord."

They also went to offer a sacrifice of a pair of doves or two young pigeons, as required by the law of the Lord. At that time there was a man named Simeon living in Jerusalem. He was a good, God-fearing man and was waiting for Israel to be saved. The Holy Spirit was with him and had assured him that he would not die before he had seen the Lord's promised Messiah. Led by the Spirit, Simeon went into the Temple. When the parents brought the child Jesus into the Temple to do for him what the Law required, Simeon took the child in his arms and gave thanks to God:

"Now, Lord, you have kept your promise, and you may let your servant go in peace. With my own eyes I have seen your salvation, which you have prepared in the presence of all peoples:
A light to reveal your will to the Gentiles
and bring glory to your people Israel."

The child's father and mother were amazed at the things Simeon said about him. Simeon blessed them and said to Mary, his mother. **"This child is chosen by God for the destruction and the salvation of many in Israel. He will be a sign from God which many people will speak against and so reveal their secret thoughts. And sorrow, like a sharp sword, will break your own heart."**

There was a very old prophetess, a widow named Anna, daughter of Phanuel of the tribe of Asher. She had been married for only seven years and was now eighty-four years old. She never left the Temple; day and night she worshiped God, fasting and praying. That very same hour she arrived and gave thanks to God and spoke about the child to all who were waiting for God to set Jerusalem free.

The Holy Bible

MATTHEW 2: 1-12
VISITORS FROM THE EAST

Jesus was born in the town of Bethlehem in Judea, during the time when Herod was king. Soon afterward, some men who studied the stars came from the East to Jerusalem and asked,

"Where is the baby born to be the king of the Jews? We saw his star when it came up in the east, and we have come to worship him."

When King Herod heard about this, he was very upset, and so was everyone else in Jerusalem. He called together all the chief priests and the teachers of the Law and asked them,

"Where will the Messiah be born?" "In the town of Bethlehem in Judea," they answered. For this is what the prophet wrote:

'Bethlehem in the land of Judah, you are by no means the least of the leading cities of Judah; for from you will come a leader who will guide my people Israel.' "

So Herod called the visitors from the East to a secret meeting and found out from them the exact time the star had appeared. Then he sent them to Bethlehem with these instructions:

"Go and make a careful search for the child; and when you find him, let me know, so that I too may go and worship him."

And so they left, and on their way they saw the same star they had seen in the East. When they saw it, how happy they were, what joy was theirs! It went ahead of them until it stopped over the place where the child was. They went into the house, and when they saw the child with his mother Mary, they knelt down and worshiped him. They brought out their gifts of gold, frankincense, and myrrh, and presented them to him.

Then they returned to their country by another road, since God had warned them in a dream not to go back to Herod.

MATTHEW 2: 13-18
THE ESCAPE TO EGYPT

After they had left, an angel of the Lord appeared in a dream to Joseph and said,

"Herod will be looking for the child in order to kill him. So get up, take the child and his mother and escape to Egypt, and stay there until I tell you to leave."

Joseph got up, took the child and his mother, and left during the night for Egypt, where he stayed until Herod died. This was done to make come true what the Lord had said through the prophet, **"I called my Son out of Egypt."**

THE KILLING OF THE CHILDREN

When Herod realized that the visitors from the East had tricked him, he was furious. He gave orders to kill all the boys in Bethlehem and its neighborhood who were two years old and younger-this was done in accordance with what he had learned from the visitors about the time when the star had appeared. In this way what the prophet Jeremiah had said came true:

"A sound is heard in Ramah, the sound of bitter weeping. Rachel is crying for her children; she refuses to be comforted, for they are dead."

MATTHEW 2: 19-23
THE RETURN FROM EGYPT

After Herod died, an angel of the Lord appeared in a dream to Joseph in Egypt and said,

"Get up, take the child and his mother, and go back to the land of Israel, because those who tried to kill the child are dead."

So Joseph got up, took the child and his mother, and went back to Israel.

But when Joseph heard that Archelaus had succeeded his father Herod as king of Judea, he was afraid to go there. He was given more instructions in a dream, so he went to the province of Galilee and made his home in a town named Nazareth. And so what the prophets had said came true:

"He will be called a Nazarene."

LUKE 2, 39-40
THE RETURN TO NAZARETH

When Joseph and Mary had finished doing all that was required by the Law of the Lord, they returned to their hometown of Nazareth in Galilee. The child grew and became strong; he was full of wisdom, and God's blessings were upon him.

The Holy Bible

LUKE 2, 41-52
THE BOY JESUS IN THE TEMPLE

Every year the parents of Jesus went to Jerusalem for the Passover Festival. When Jesus was twelve years old, they went to the festival as usual. When the festival was over, they started back home, but the boy Jesus stayed in Jerusalem. His parents did not know this; they thought that he was with the group, so they traveled a whole day and then started looking for him among their relatives and friends. They did not find him, so they went back to Jerusalem looking for him. On the third day they found him in the Temple, sitting with the Jewish teachers, listening to them and asking questions. All who heard him were amazed at his intelligent answers. His parents were astonished when they saw him, and his mother said to him,

"Son, why have you done this to us? Your father and I have been terribly worried trying to find you."

He answered them,

"Why did you have to look for me? Didn't you know that I had to be in my Father's house?"

But they did not understand his answer. So Jesus went back with them to Nazareth, where he was obedient to them. His mother treasured all these things in her heart. Jesus grew both in body and in wisdom, gaining favor with God and men.

PALESTINE IN THE TIME OF JESUS

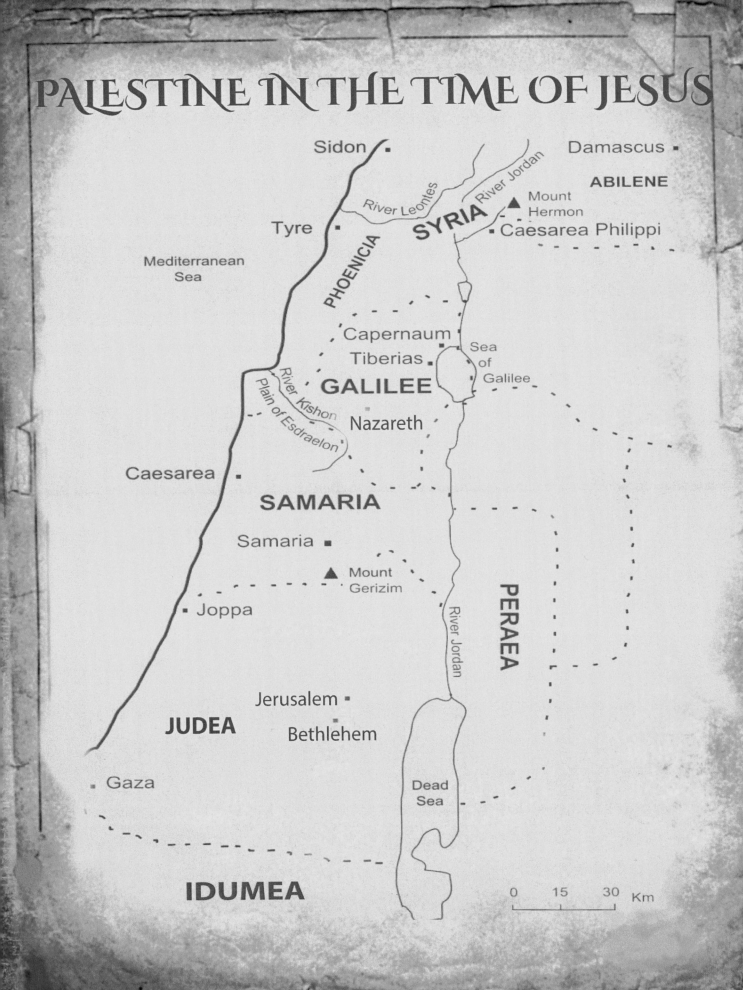

Sidon

Damascus

River Leontes

River Jordan

ABILENE

Mount Hermon

Tyre

SYRIA

Caesarea Philippi

PHOENICIA

Mediterranean Sea

Capernaum

Sea of Galilee

Tiberias

GALILEE

River Kishon

Plain of Esdraelon

Nazareth

Caesarea

SAMARIA

Samaria

Mount Gerizim

PERAEA

Joppa

River Jordan

Jerusalem

JUDEA

Bethlehem

Gaza

Dead Sea

IDUMEA

0   15   30   Km

The Holy Bible

MATTHEW 1: 1-17
THE ANCESTORS OF JESUS CHRIST

This is the list of the ancestors of Jesus Christ, a descendant of David, who was a descendant of Abraham. From Abraham to King David, the following ancestors are listed: Abraham, Isaac, Jacob, Judah and his brothers; then Perez and Zerah (their mother was Tamar), Hezron, Ram, Amminadab, Nahshon, Salmon, Boaz (his mother was Rahab), Obed (his mother was Ruth), Jesse, and King David.

From David to the time when the people of Israel were taken into exile in Babylon, the following ancestors are listed: David, Solomon (his mother was the woman who had been Uriah's wife), Rehoboam, Abijah, Asa, Jehoshaphat, Jehoram, Uzziah, Jotham, Ahaz, Hezekiah, Manasseh, Amon, Josiah, and Jehoiachin and his brothers.

From the time after the exile in Babylon to the birth of Jesus, the following ancestors are listed: Jehoiachin, Shealtiel, Zerubbabel, Abiud, Eliakim, Azor, Zadok, Achim, Eliud, Eleazar, Matthan, Jacob, and Joseph, who married Mary, the mother of Jesus, who was called the Messiah.

So then, there were fourteen generations from Abraham to David, and fourteen from David to the exile in Babylon, and fourteen from then to the birth of the Messiah.

The Word of the Lord

Thanks be to God

Amen

The Holy Bible

JOHN I, 1-18
THE WORD OF LIFE

Before the world was created, the Word already existed; he was with God, and he was the same as God. From the very beginning the Word was with God. Through him God made all things; not one thing in all creation was made without him. The Word was the source of life, and this life brought light to mankind. The light shines in the darkness, and the darkness has never put it out.

God sent his messenger, a man named John, who came to tell people about the light, so that all should hear the message and believe. He himself was not the light; he came to tell about the light. This was the real light-the light that comes into the world and shines on all mankind.

The word was in the world, and though God made the world through him, yet the world did not recognize him. He came to his own country, but his own people did not receive him. Some, however, did receive him and believed in him; so he gave them the right to become God's children. They did not become God's children by natural means, that is, by being born as the children of a human father; God himself was their Father. The Word became a human being and, full of grace and truth, lived among us. We saw his glory, the glory which he received as the Father's only Son. John spoke about him. He cried out,

"This is the one I was talking about when I said, 'He comes after me, but he is greater than I am, because he existed before I was born.'"

Out of the fullness of his grace he has blessed us all, giving us one blessing after another. God gave the Law through Moses, but grace and truth came through Jesus Christ. No one has ever seen God. The only Son who is the same as God and is at the Father's side, he has made him known.

Epilogue

Jesus lived on earth for thirty-three years. He lived with his parents, Mary and Joseph, and worked with his father, who was a carpenter. At age thirty, he began his ministry, which lasted only three years. During that time He preached about God being our Father who knows us intimately and loves us. Jesus taught us about The Kingdom of God and how we should live and keep His Commandments; not out of fear but because we love God. These Commandments were meant to keep us free from sin and safe from the dangers of evil.

Jesus taught us to love one another as we love ourselves. He taught us to help each other and give what we can without expecting anything in return. Jesus taught this by example as He suffered and laid down His life for us so that we might have life everlasting. People came from far away to hear Him speak. He was sought after and had thousands of followers and disciples. Jesus called His twelve Apostles who left everything they had to follow Him. There were many people who were healed by His countless miracles. When people heard of His miracles they believed and brought all who needed healing to Him. Jesus is the same yesterday, today and tomorrow therefore He continues to heal, forgive and give hope to whomever comes to Him.

Jesus died at the age of thirty-three he was severely beaten, crowned with thorns that pierced his head, and died by being crucified. His mother, Mary, stood at the foot of His cross. On the third day after his death; he rose from the dead in fulfillment of the Scriptures.

The Apostles and disciples continued the teachings of Jesus Christ, and Christianity spread throughout the world. Many people were killed because of their faith in Jesus. They would rather suffer and die, than to renounce their Christianity.

Today, as disciples of Jesus, we must live as He taught us by His words and examples even when His teachings are difficult to follow. As Christians we are called to forgive those whose cause us harm and to pray for them. Jesus is asking us to be humble and obedient. He is asking us to give of ourselves unselfishly to others.

Living our Catholic faith means to not only follow God's Commandments, but to give up everything and follow Christ even on to death. It is this gift of faith that allows us to surrender our lives to Jesus so we, in turn, have something to live for. The real meaning of life is that we were made to love and serve the Lord and be with God for eternity.

Traditional Catholic Prayers

The Gift of an
All Catholic Christmas

Litany of
The Blessed Virgin Mary

*We can know
the Blessed Virgin Mary and St. Joseph better
by reciting their litanies.
These are the other names or titles that Christians through
the ages have referred to them.*

Litany of
St. Joseph

The Gift of an
All Catholic Christmas

Litany of
The Blessed Virgin Mary

Verse

Lord, have mercy on us.
Lord, have mercy on us.

Christ, hear us.
God the Father of Heaven,
God the Son, Redeemer of the
world,
God the Holy Spirit,
Holy Trinity, One God,

Holy Mary,
Holy Mother of God,
Holy Virgin of virgins,
Mother of Christ,
Mother of divine grace,
Mother most pure,
Mother most chaste,
Mother inviolate,
Mother undefiled,
Mother most amiable,
Mother most admirable,
Mother of good counsel,
Mother of our Creator,
Mother of our Savior,
Mother of the Church,
Virgin most prudent,

Response

Christ have mercy on us.

Christ, graciously hear us.
Have mercy on us.

Have mercy on us.
Have mercy on us.
Have mercy on us.

Pray for us.
Pray for us.
Pray for us.
Pray for us.
Pray for us.
Pray for us.
Pray for us.
Pray for us.
Pray for us.
Pray for us.
Pray for us.
Pray for us.
Pray for us.
Pray for us.
Pray for us.
Pray for us.

Litany of
The Blessed Virgin Mary
Continued

Verse	*Response*
Virgin most venerable,	pray for us.
Virgin most renowned,	pray for us.
Virgin most powerful,	pray for us.
Virgin most merciful,	pray for us.
Virgin most faithful,	pray for us.
Mirror of justice,	pray for us.
Seat of wisdom,	pray for us.
Cause of our joy,	pray for us.
Spiritual vessel,	pray for us.
Vessel of honor,	pray for us.
Singular vessel of devotion,	pray for us.
Mystical rose,	pray for us.
Tower of David,	pray for us.
Tower of ivory,	pray for us.
House of gold,	pray for us.
Ark of the covenant,	pray for us.
Gate of Heaven,	pray for us.
Morning star,	pray for us.
Health of the sick,	pray for us.
Refuge of sinners,	pray for us.
Comforter of the afflicted,	pray for us.
Help of Christians,	pray for us.
Queen of angels,	pray for us.
Queen of patriarchs,	pray for us.
Queen of prophets	pray for us.
Queen of apostles,	pray for us.

Litany of
The Blessed Virgin Mary
Continued

Verse	*Response*
Queen of martyrs,	pray for us.
Queen of confessors,	pray for us.
Queen of virgins,	pray for us.
Queen of all saints,	pray for us.
Queen conceived without	pray for us.
Original Sin,	pray for us.
Queen assumed into Heaven,	pray for us.
Queen of the Holy Rosary,	pray for us.
Queen of families,	pray for us.
Queen of peace,	pray for us.
Lamb of God, Who takes away the sins of the world,	Spare us, O Lord.
Lamb of God, Who takes away the sins of the world,	Graciously hear us, O Lord.
Lamb of God, Who takes away the sins of the world,	Have Mercy on us.
Pray for us, O holy Mother of God,	That we may be made worthy of the promises of Christ.

The Gift of an
All Catholic Christmas

Litany of St. Joseph

Verse

Lord, have mercy.
Christ have mercy.
Lord, have mercy.

Jesus, hear us.

God, the Father of Heaven,
God, the Son, Redeemer of the world.
God, the Holy Spirit,
Holy Trinity, One God,
Holy Mary,
St. Joseph,
Renowned offspring of David,
Light of Patriarchs,
Spouse of the Mother of God,
Chaste guardian of the Virgin,
Foster father of the Son of God,
Diligent protector of Christ,
Head of the Holy Family,
Joseph most just,
Joseph most chaste,
Joseph most prudent,
Joseph most strong,
Joseph most obedient,
Joseph most faithful,
Mirror of patience,
Lover of poverty,

Response

Lord, have mercy.
Christ, have mercy.
Lord, have mercy.

Jesus graciously hear us.

Have mercy on us.
Have mercy on us.
Have mercy on us.
Have mercy on us.
pray for us.
pray for us.
pray for us.
pray for us.
pray for us.
pray for us.
pray for us.
pray for us.
pray for us.
pray for us.
pray for us.
pray for us.
pray for us.
pray for us.
pray for us.
pray for us.
pray for us.

Litany of St. Joseph
Continued

Verse	*Response*
Model of workmen,	pray for us.
Glory of home life,	pray for us.
Guardian of virgins,	pray for us.
Pillar of families,	pray for us.
Solace of the wretched,	pray for us.
Hope of the sick,	pray for us.
Patron of the dying,	pray for us.
Terror of demons,	pray for us.
Protector of Holy Church,	pray for us.
Lamb of God, who takes away the sins of the world.	spare us, O Lord.
Lamb of God, who takes away the sins of the world.	graciously hear us, O Lord.
Lamb of God, who takes away the sins of the world.	have mercy on us.

He made him the lord of his household and prince over all his possessions.

Let us pray - O God, Who in Thy divine providence chose Blessed Saint Joseph to be the spouse of Thy most Holy Mother Mary; grant we beseech Thee, that he may serve as our intercessor in Heaven, just as he serves as our protector here on earth. We ask this through your Son, our Lord Jesus Christ, who lives and reigns with You and the Holy Spirit, one God, forever and ever. Amen.

The Gift of an
All Catholic Christmas

We relive the miracle of the
birth of Jesus when we say:

The Angelus Prayer

Verse
Response

The Angel of the Lord declared unto Mary,
And she conceived of the Holy Spirit.

(say one Hail Mary Prayer)

Verse
Response

Behold the handmaid of the Lord.
Be it done unto me according to Your Word.

(say one Hail Mary Prayer)

Verse
Response

And the Word was made flesh,
And dwelt among us.

(say one Hail Mary Prayer)

Verse
Response

Pray for us, O holy Mother of God.
That we may be made worthy of the promises of Christ.

Let us pray:
Pour forth, we beseech You, O Lord,
Your Grace into our hearts;
that as we have known the incarnation of Christ,
your Son by the message of an angel,
so by His passion and cross
we may be brought to the glory of His Resurrection.
Through the same Christ, our Lord.
Amen.

(The Angelus is said by Catholics all over the world, everyday at twelve o'clock noon.)

We meditate on the birth of Jesus when we recite:

The Five Joyful Mysteries
Of the Most Holy Rosary

Ten Hail Mary's

On this bead say:

Glory Be to the Father

The Fatima Prayer

The Fourth Joyful Mystery

"The Presentation"

The Our Father

The Presentation
Fourth Joyful Mystery

The Birth of Jesus
Third Joyful Mystery

On this bead say:

Glory Be to the Father

The Fatima Prayer

The Third Joyful Mystery

"The Birth of Jesus"

The Our Father

Ten Hail Mary's

The Finding of Jesus in the Temple
Fifth Joyful Mystery

The Annunciation
First Joyful Mystery

The Visitation
Second Joyful Mystery

On this bead say:

Glory Be to the Father

The Fatima Prayer

The Fifth Joyful Mystery

"The Finding of Jesus in the Temple"

The Our Father

Ten Hail Mary's

On this bead say:

Glory Be to the Father

The Fatima Prayer

The Second Joyful Mystery

"The Visitation"

The Our Father

Ten Hail Mary's

Glory Be to the Father

The Fatima Prayer

Hail Holy Queen

Let us Pray

The Memorare

St. Michael

Three Hail Mary's

On this bead say: Glory Be to the Father

The First Joyful Mystery

"The Annunciation"

The Our Father

On this bead say:
The Apostles Creed and The Our Father

At the beginning and at the end of the rosary make and recite the Sign of the Cross while holding the crucifix.

50

We meditate on the birth of Jesus when we recite:
The Five Joyful Mysteries
Of the Most Holy Rosary

The angel came to her and said, "Peace be with you!
The Lord is with you and has greatly blessed you!"...
The angel said to her,
"Don't be afraid, Mary; God has been gracious to you.

Luke 1:28, 30

When Elizabeth heard Mary's greeting, the baby moved within her.
Elizabeth was filled with the Holy Spirit and said in a loud voice,
"You are the most blessed of all women, and blessed is the child you will bear!

Luke 1:41-42

She gave birth to her first son, wrapped him in cloths and laid him in a
manger—there was no room for them to stay in the inn.

Luke 2:7

The time came for Joseph and Mary to perform the ceremony of purification,
as the Law of Moses commanded. So they took the child to Jerusalem
to present him to the Lord,

Luke 2:22

On the third day they found him in the Temple,
sitting with the Jewish teachers, listening to them and asking questions.

Luke 2:46

The following pages contain the prayers of the Most Holy Rosary.

Sign of the Cross

In the Name of the Father,
And the Son,
And the Holy Spirit,

Amen.

Apostle's Creed

I believe in God, the Father almighty, creator of heaven and
earth. I believe in Jesus Christ, his only Son, our Lord.
He was conceived by the power of the Holy Spirit and born of
the Virgin Mary. He suffered under Pontius Pilate, was
crucified, died, and was buried. He descended into hell.
On the third day he rose again. He ascended into heaven
and is seated at the right hand of the Father. He will come
again to judge the living and the dead.

I believe in the Holy Spirit, the Holy Catholic Church,
the communion of saints, the forgiveness of sins,
the resurrection of the body, and the life everlasting.
Amen.

The Our Father

Our Father,
Who art in Heaven,
hallowed be Thy name; Thy Kingdom come,
Thy will be done on earth as it is in Heaven.
Give us this day our daily bread; and forgive us
our trespasses as we forgive those
who trespass against us; and lead us not
into temptation, but deliver us from evil.

Amen.

Hail Mary

Hail Mary, full of Grace,
the Lord is with thee.
Blessed art thou among women
and blessed is the fruit of thy womb, Jesus.
Holy Mary, Mother of God,
pray for us sinners, now, and at the
hour of our death.

Amen.

Glory Be to the Father

Glory be to the Father,
and to the Son,
and to the Holy Spirit.
As it was in the beginning,
is now,
and ever shall be,
world without end.

Amen.

The Fatima Prayer

O my Jesus, forgive us our sins,
save us from the fires of hell,
lead all souls to heaven,
especially those who are
in most need of Thy mercy.

Amen.

Hail Holy Queen

Hail, holy Queen, mother of mercy, our life,
our sweetness, and our hope.
To thee do we cry, poor banished children of Eve.
To thee do we send up our sighs,
mourning and weeping in this valley of tears.
Turn then, most gracious advocate,
thine eyes of mercy toward us,
and after this our exile, show unto
us the blessed fruit of thy womb, Jesus.
O clement, O loving, O sweet Virgin Mary!

Pray for us, O Holy Mother of God,
that we may be made worthy of the promises of Christ.

Let us Pray

O God, whose only begotten Son, by His life, death,
and resurrection, has purchased for us the rewards of eternal salvation.
Grant, we beseech Thee, that while meditating on these mysteries
of the most holy Rosary of the Blessed Virgin Mary,
we may imitate what they contain and obtain
what they promise, through Christ our Lord. Amen.

Most Sacred Heart of Jesus, have mercy on us.

Immaculate Heart of Mary, pray for us.

Amen.

Memorare

Remember, O most gracious Virgin Mary,
that never was it known that anyone
who fled to thy protection,
implored thy help, or sought
thy intercession, was left unaided.
Inspired with this confidence,
I fly unto thee,
O Virgin of virgins, my Mother.
To thee do I come, before thee I stand,
sinful and sorrowful.
O Mother of the Word Incarnate,
despise not my petitions,
but in thy mercy, hear and answer me.

Amen.

Saint Michael, the Archangel

St. Michael the Archangel,
defend us in battle.
Be our defense against the
wickedness and snares of the devil.
May God rebuke him, we humbly pray,
and do thou,
O Prince of the heavenly host,
by the divine power of God,
thrust into hell satan,
and all the evil spirits,
who prowl about the world
seeking the ruin of souls.

Amen.

The Gift of an

All Catholic Christmas

Holy

Christmas

Songs

Holy Christmas Songs

Christmas Song 1	Silent Night
Christmas Song 2	Away In a Manger
Christmas Song 3	What Child is This
Christmas Song 4	O Little Town of Bethlehem
Christmas Song 5	O Come, O Come Emmanuel
Christmas Song 6	It Came Upon A Midnight Clear
Christmas Song 7	Joy to the World
Christmas Song 8	God Rest Ye Merry Gentlemen
Christmas Song 9	Hark The Herald Angels Sing
Christmas Song 10	Angels We Have Heard on High
Christmas Song 11	The First Noel
Christmas Song 12	O Come All Ye Faithful
Christmas Song 13	We Three Kings

Sing to the Lord, all the world!
Worship the Lord with joy;
come before him with happy songs!

Psalm 100:1-2

Silent Night

1. Silent night, holy night! All is calm, all is bright.
2. Silent night, holy night! Shepherds quake at the sight.
3. Silent night, holy night! Son of God love's pure light.

1. Round yon Virgin, Mother and Child.
2. Glories stream from heaven afar
3. Radiant beams from Thy holy face

1. Holy infant so tender and mild,
2. Heavenly hosts sing Alleluia,
3. With dawn of redeeming grace,

1. Sleep in heavenly peace, Sleep in heavenly peace.
2. Christ the Savior is born! Christ the Savior is born.
3. Jesus Lord, at Thy birth, Jesus Lord, at Thy birth.

Away In a Manger

1. Away in a manger, No crib for His bed,
2. The cattle are lowing, The poor Baby wakes,
3. Be near me, Lord Jesus, I ask Thee to stay,

1. The little Lord Jesus, Lay down his sweet head.
2. But little Lord Jesus, No crying He makes;
3. Close by me forever, And love me I pray!

1. The Stars in the sky, Looked down where He lay
2. I love Thee, Lord Jesus, Look down from the sky
3. Bless all the dear children, In Thy tender care

1. The little Lord Jesus, Asleep on the hay.
2. And stay by my cradle Till morning is nigh.
3. And take us to heaven, To live with thee there.

What Child is This

1. What Child is this who, laid to rest on Mary's
2. Why lies He in such mean estate, Where ox
3. So bring Him incense, gold and myrrh, Come peasant

1. lap is sleeping? Whom Angels greet with anthems sweet,
2. and ass are feeding? Good Christians, fear for sinners hear
3. king to own Him; The King of kings salvation brings,

1. While shepherds watch are keeping?
2. The silent Word is pleading.
3. Let loving hearts enthrone Him.

(Refrain 1-3)
This, this is Christ the King, Whom shepherds guard
and Angels sing; Haste, haste to bring Him laud,
The Babe, the Son of Mary.

O Little Town of Bethlehem

1. O little town of Bethlehem, How still we see thee lie!
2. For Christ is born of Mary, And gathered all above
3. How silently, how silently, The wondrous gift is given;
4. O holy Child of Bethlehem, Descend to us, we pray!

1. Above thy deep and dreamless sleep The silent stars go by.
2. While mortals sleep, the angels keep Their watch of wond'ring love.
3. So God imparts to human hearts The blessings of His Heaven.
4. Cast out our sin and enter in, Be born to us today.

1. Yet in the dark streets shineth. The everlasting Light
2. O morning stars, together Proclaim the holy birth!
3. No ear may hear His coming, But in this world of sin,
4. We hear the Christmas angels, The great glad tidings tell;

1. The hopes and fears of all the years, are met in thee tonight.
2. And praises sing to God the King, And peace to men on earth.
3. Where meek souls will receive Him still, The dear Christ enters in.
4. O come to us, abide with us, Our Lord Emmanuel!

O Come, O Come, Emmanuel

1. O come, O come Emmanuel,
2. O come, Thou Wisdom from on high,
3. O come, O come, Thou Lord of might,
4. O come, Thou Rod of Jesse's stem,

1. And ransom captive Israel,
2. Who ord'rest all things mightily;
3. Who to thy tribe on Sinai's height
4. From every foe deliver them

1. That mourns in lonely exile here
2. To us the past of knowledge show,
3. In ancient times didst give the law,
4. That trust thy mighty pow'r to save,

1. Until the Son of God appear.
2. And teach us in her ways to go.
3. In cloud and majesty and awe.
4. And give them vict'ry o'er the grave.

Refrain 1-3
Rejoice! Rejoice! Emmanual
Shall come to thee, O Israel!

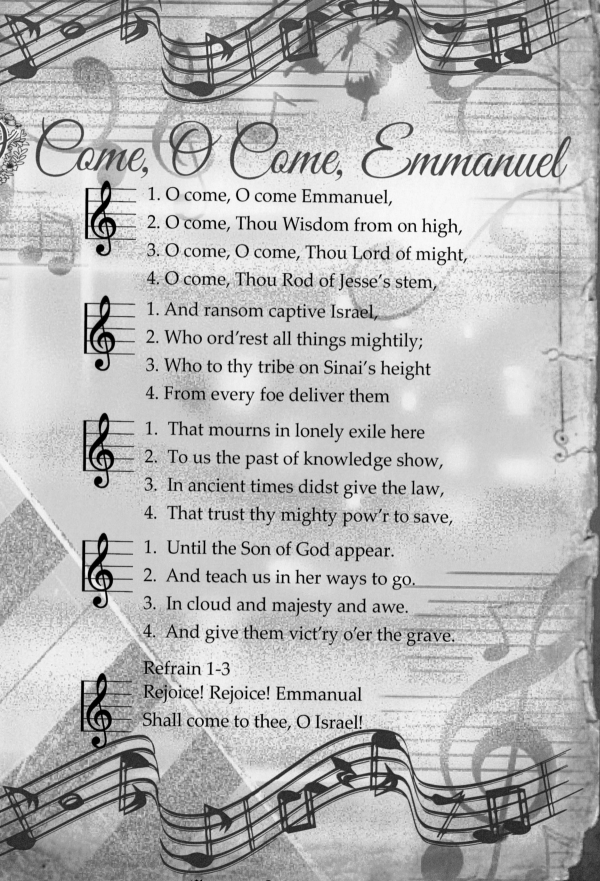

It Came Upon A Midnight Clear

1. It came upon the midnight clear, That glorious song of old,

2. Still through the cloven skies they come With peaceful wings unfurled

3. For lo! The days are hastening on, By prophet bards foretold,

1. From angels bending near the earth To touch their harps of gold!

2. And still their heavenly music floats O'er all the weary world;

3. When, with the ever-circling years, Shall come the Age of Gold;

1. "Peace on the earth, good will to men,"

2. Above its sad and lowly plains

3. When peace shall over all the earth

1. From heaven's all gracious King!

2. They bend on hovering wing.

3. Its ancient splendors fling,

1. The world in solemn stillness lay To hear the angels sing.

2. And ever o'er its Babel sounds The Blessed angels sing.

3. And all the world give back the song Which now the angels sing.

Joy to the World

1. Joy to the world! The Lord is come; Let earth receive her King'
2. Joy to the earth! The Savior reigns; Let us their songs employ;
3. He rules the world with truth and grace, And makes the nations prove

1. Let every heart prepare Him room,
2. While fields and floods, Rocks, hills and plains
3. The glories of His righteousness,

1. And heaven and nature sing, And heaven and nature sing,
2. Repeat the sounding joy, Repeat the sounding joy,
3. And wonders of His love, And wonders of His love,

1. And heaven, and heaven and nature sing.
2. Repeat, repeat the sounding joy.
3. And wonders, wonders of His love.

God Rest Ye Merry, Gentlemen

1. God rest ye merry, gentlemen Let nothing you dismay

2. From God our Heavenly Father A blessed Angel came;

3. "Fear not then, " said the Angel, "Let nothing you affright,

4. Now to the Lord sing praises, All you within this place,

1. Remember, Christ , our Savior Was born on Christmas day

2. This day is born a Savior Of a pure Virgin Bright,

3. Close by me forever, And love me I pray!

4. And with true love and brotherhood Each other now embrace;

1. To save us all from satan's power When we were gone astray.

2. How that in Bethlehem was born The Son of God by Name.

3. To free all those who trust in Him From satan's power and might."

4. This holy tide of Christmas All other doth deface.

Refrain 1-4

O tidings of comfort and joy, Comfort and joy

O tidings of comfort and joy.

Hark! The Herald Angels Sing

1. Hark! The Herald Angels sing, "Glory to the new-born King.
2. Christ by highest Heaven ador'd, Christ the everlasting Lord!
3. Hail the Heaven-born Prince of Peace! Hail the Son of righteousness!

1. Peace on earth, and mercy mild, God and sinners reconciled!"
2. Late in time behold him come, Offspring of a Virgin's womb.
3. Light and life to all he brings, Risen with healing in his wings.

1. Joyful all ye nations rise, Join the triumph of the skies,
2. Veiled in flesh the God-head see! Hail th'incarnate Deity!
3. Mild he lays his glory by, Born that we no more may die,

1. With the angelic host proclaim, Christ is born in Bethlehem.
2. Pleased as man with us to dwell; Jesus our Emmanuel!
3. Born to raise us from the earth, Born to give us second birth.

Refrain 1-3

Hark the herald angels sing, "Glory to the newborn King."

Angels We Have Heard on High

1. Angels we have heard on high
2. Shepherds, why this jubilee?
3. Come to Bethlehem and see
4. See Him in a manger laid,

1. Sweetly singing o'er the plains,
2. Why your joyous strains prolong?
3. Christ Whose birth the angels sing;
4. Whom the choirs of angels praise;

1. And the mountains in reply
2. What the gladsome tidings be
3. Come, adore on bended knee,
4. Mary, Joseph, lend your aid,

1. Echoing their joyous strains.
2. Which inspire your heavenly song?
3. Christ the Lord, the newborn King.
4. While our hearts in love we raise.

Refrain 1-4

Gloria, in excelsis Deo! Gloria, in excelsis Deo!

The First Noel

1. The first Noel the angel did say
2. They looked up and saw a star
3. And by the light of that same star
4. This star drew nigh to the north west,
5. Then entered in those wise men three
6. Then Let us all with one accord

1. Was to certain poor shepherds In fields as they lay;
2. Shining in the east beyond them far,
3. Three wise men came from country far;
4. O'er Bethlehem it took it rest,
5. Full reverently upon their knee,
6. Sing praises to our heavenly Lord;

1. In fields as they lay, keeping their sheep,
2. And to the earth it gave great light,
3. To seek for a king was their intent,
4. And there it did both stop and stay
5. And offered there in his presence
6. Sing praises to our heavenly Lord;

1. On a cold winter's night that was so deep.
2. And so it continued both day and night.
3. And to follow the star wherever it went.
4. Right over the place where Jesus lay.
5. Their gold, and myrrh, and frankincense.
6. .And with his blood mankind hath bought.

Refrain 1-6

Noel, Noel, Noel, Noel, Born is the King of Israel

Christmas Song 11

O Come All Ye Faithful

1. O come, all ye faithful, Joyful and triumphant,
2. Sing, choirs of angels, Sing in exultation;
3. Yea, Lord, we greet Thee, Born this happy morning;

1. O come ye, O come ye, to Bethlehem.
2. Sing, all ye citizens of heaven above!
3. Jesus, to Thee be glory given;

1. Come and behold Him, Born the King of angels;
2. Glory to God, In the highest;
3. Word of the Father, Now in flesh appearing.

Refrain 1-3
O come, let us adore Him,
O come, let us adore Him,
O come, let us adore Him,
Christ the Lord.

We Three Kings

1. We three kings of Orient are; Bearing gifts we traverse afar
2. Born a King on Bethlehem's plain, Gold I bring to crown him again;
3. Frankincense to offer have I: Incense owns a Deity nigh;
4. Myrrh is mine; its bitter perfume Breathes a life of gathering gloom;
5. Glorious now, be-hold him arise, King and God and Sacrifice;

1. Field and Fountain, Moor and mountain, Following yonder star.
2. King forever, Ceasing never Over us all to reign.
3. Pray'r and praising Gladly raising, Worshiping him God on high.
4. Sorr'wing sighing, Bleeding, dying, Sealed in the stone-cold tomb.
5. "Alleluia, Alleluia!" Sounds through the earth and skies.

Refrain 1-5
O star of wonder, star of night, Star with royal beauty bright,
Westward leading, still proceeding, Guide us to thy perfect light.

The Gift of an
All Catholic Christmas

Christmas reflections:

Elli's Page

Many people think Christmas is a day about presents, but it's not, it's actually the day Jesus is born. It's the day we celebrate the day God's son was born on the earth. He was put in a manger by Mary, the Holy Mother of Jesus.

Elli, Age 10

The Gift of an
All Catholic Christmas

Christmas reflections:

The Gift of an
All Catholic Christmas

Christmas reflections:

The Gift of an All Catholic Christmas

Christmas reflections:

Acknowledge that the Lord is God.
He made us, and we belong to him;
we are his people, we are his flock.
Enter the Temple gates with thanksgiving;
go into its courts with praise
Give thanks to him and praise him.
The Lord is good; his love is eternal
and his faithfulness lasts forever.

Psalms 100: 3-5